the *AIRPLANE* *book*

the AIRPLANE *book*

Cheryl Walsh Bellville

Carolrhoda Books, Inc./Minneapolis

To my dad, Lt. Col. Wm. V. Walsh, USAF (Ret.)

Front cover: C-45 Beechcraft cargo plane
Back cover inset: F-16 Flying Falcon jet
Page one: RF-84F Thunderjet
Page two: British Tri-Motor over the Gulf of Mexico

LIBRARY OF CONGRESS CATALOGING-IN-PUBLICATION DATA

Bellville, Cheryl Walsh.
   The airplane book / by Cheryl Walsh Bellville.
    p.   cm.
   Includes index.
   Summary: Highlights airplanes of the last 100 years and discusses the principles of flight, early aviation, the growth of modern airliners, and current design challenges.
   ISBN 0-87614-686-8 (lib. bdg.)
   1. Airplanes — Juvenile literature. [1. Airplanes.] I. Title.
TL547.B395   1991
629.133'34 — dc20   91-10522
                                                  CIP
                                                    AC

Manufactured in the United States of America

1 2 3 4 5 6 7 8 9 10 00 99 98 97 96 95 94 93 92 91

Did you ever lie on your back on a hillside looking up at the summer sky? Were you lost for a while imagining yourself moving across the sky with the clouds? I have, and I'll bet you have, too.

I grew up on air force bases where airplanes were as common as cars and trucks. This short history of airplanes was inspired by my childhood on air bases and my love of flying. In this book, I will introduce you to some of my favorite planes.

People have always dreamed of flying. At first, people thought they could fly by strapping wings to their arms and flapping them as a bird does. A hundred years ago in Germany, Otto Lilienthal had a better idea. He built gliders, motorless aircraft that used the movement of air to stay aloft.

In the 1890s, Otto Lilienthal launched his gliders by jumping from a hillside he made for that purpose.

Lift helped Lilienthal's gliders fly. When air flows over and around a curved wing, it lifts the wing up. Birds use lift to soar and glide through the air. Lilienthal studied birds and built gliders shaped like birds' wings. He made more than 2,000 flights, and was just about to put a motor on one of his gliders when he died in a crash.

Modern gliders, sometimes called sailplanes, move smoothly through the air. The silent sport of gliding may be the closest we can come to the flight of birds.

The Wright brothers flew their gliders like kites, holding onto them with cables.

In the United States, two brothers named Wilbur and Orville Wright read about Lilienthal's work. They used some of Otto Lilienthal's ideas and some of their own to build gliders that looked more like box kites than birds' wings. Later, the Wright brothers flew their gliders with a person aboard. By 1902, they were ready to add an engine.

Orville Wright won a coin toss with his brother Wilbur and piloted the Flyer *on its first successful flight.*

The problem was, there were no engines light enough to put on a glider. The Wright brothers worked on this problem with their shop mechanic and built their own lightweight gasoline engine.

The engine powered two **propellers** on the 1903 Wright *Flyer*. These propellers faced backward and pushed the aircraft forward. The force that pushed the *Flyer* forward is called **thrust**.

The Wright *Flyer* was a **biplane**, a plane with two sets of wings, one above the other. The plane was made of cloth and wood, so it was very lightweight. What we might think of as a tail was placed in front of the wings and was used to turn the plane. The angle of the wings was changed by pulling wires, a device the Wright brothers called "wing warping." Wing warping helped the Wright brothers to control the *Flyer* and to prevent the plane from rolling from side to side.

On December 17, 1903, the Wright *Flyer* lifted off the ground and flew 120 feet. The age of motorized flight had begun.

The airplane was only 10 years old when the First World War broke out in Europe. Airplanes were used for checking the position of enemy troops, or **reconnaissance**. In those early days of the war, there was an unwritten rule among flyers never to harm another pilot. One day in 1914, however, a corporal flying in a French biplane shot down a German plane. After that, airplanes became weapons of war.

Not long before World War I, Wilbur Wright shipped a Flyer *to France where he demonstrated his flight skills and frightened horses.*

At first, World War I air battles were ruled by the Fokker Eindekker, a German plane. It shot down so many planes, it became known as the Fokker Scourge.

Eindekker means "one wing" in German. Airplanes with one set of wings, called **monoplanes**, are generally faster than biplanes. They have fewer wires, supporting **struts**, and other surfaces to resist wind and create **drag**. Drag slows down a plane. The Fokker, a very fast plane for that time, had a top speed of 80 miles per hour (mph).

By 1917, the German air force met its match in British planes such as the Sopwith Camel. This fighter plane was called the Camel because its two machine guns were mounted on a hump in front of the pilot. It was fast and well armed, but difficult and dangerous to fly.

When World War I ended in 1918, thousands of pilots were out of work. Many American pilots became **barnstormers**. Barnstormers were men and women who did stunt flying in cities and small towns across the United States. These daredevils walked on the wings of their planes, jumped from one plane to another in midair, flew upside down, and performed mock battles.

Many barnstormers flew Curtiss JN-4s, better known as Jennies. During the war, Jennies were used to train pilots for the Army Air Service. The army had thousands of Jennies, some still unassembled and in boxes, left over after the war. These war surplus planes sold for around $400, giving many people a chance to buy their own airplane.

Wood, wires, and cloth were the basic materials for all early airplanes, including this 1914 Rumpler Taube monoplane.

A young woman hangs from the wing of her Curtiss JN-4, often called a Jenny.

By the 1930s, cockpits had instruments, like the ones in this Stinson Reliant, that could be used for navigation.

Some former military pilots found jobs after the war with the new airmail service. Flying from town to town was a real adventure for these early airmail carriers. There were few airports, and most runways were no more than flat, grass fields. Most pilots flew in open **cockpits**. They were exposed to the weather and to oil leaking from the engine. Pilots wore long scarves to wipe engine oil from their goggles so they could see.

Navigation, or finding the way from one place to another, wasn't easy. Pilots leaned out of the cockpit to look down at the ground for roads, railroad tracks, and rivers. They compared what they saw to standard road maps. Sometimes there were accidents because pilots were so busy looking down at the ground for their position that they didn't see another plane flying right at them.

In 1927, a young pilot named Charles Lindbergh tried something no one else had done before. He flew alone and nonstop across the Atlantic Ocean from New York to Paris, France.

Lindbergh's *Spirit of Saint Louis* was a high-wing Ryan monoplane. The wings were placed over the body of the plane, or **fuselage**. Large fuel tanks needed for the long flight took up most of the front end of the airplane. The tanks blocked Lindbergh's view, so he had to fly by looking out side windows or by peering through a periscope.

The Stinson Reliant SR9E was nicknamed the Gullwing, because of the seagull-like arch of its wings.

Lindbergh's flight helped convince people that airplanes could fly long distances safely. For the first time, factories in the United States built airplanes designed especially for carrying passengers. Early airlines appeared on the scene and bought the new passenger airplanes, called airliners.

Some pilots for the new airlines trained in the Stinson Reliant SR9E. The Reliant was very modern looking for its time. It had an enclosed cockpit and rounded metal covers called **cowlings** around the engine. Cowling the outside edges of an airplane engine is a method of streamlining. Even the wheels of the Reliant were covered to reduce drag by helping air flow smoothly over the surface of the plane.

With luck, a new airline pilot of the 1930s might get to fly a DC-3, one of the best-loved airplanes ever built. The DC-3 has two powerful engines, one on each wing. The wings are attached to the lower part of the fuselage, making the DC-3 a low-wing monoplane.

The Douglas DC-3 first flew on December 17, 1935, thirty-two years to the day after the Wright brothers made their first motorized flight. It was an immediate success with pilots. They said the DC-3 was a "forgiving" airplane, one that would forgive a pilot for mistakes and would fly easily in bad weather or with a heavy load. Over 10,000 DC-3s were built, and hundreds are still in service around the world.

The United States entered World War II in 1941 and trained more than a million pilots. The Stearman, an open cockpit plane from the 1930s, was a primary trainer, the first airplane a student pilot flew. Stearmans were often painted yellow to make them more visible. The planes were then called the Yellow Perils because student pilots could be dangerous.

After learning to fly a Stearman, new pilots moved on to a basic trainer such as the BT-13. (*BT* stands for basic trainer.) The BT-13 had a closed cockpit, but it was still a very noisy plane to fly. Its nickname was the Vibrator, and it did.

At the beginning of the war, the United States' top fighter was the P-40 Warhawk. (*P* stands for pursuit.) P-40 Warhawks flew against Japanese fighters during the attack on Pearl Harbor, the battle that brought the United States into World War II.

This World War II P-40 Warhawk is painted in the colors of the Flying Tigers Squadron. The symbols by the cockpit show how many enemy planes the Warhawk shot down.

The B-29's wingspan of 141 feet is over 20 feet longer than the total distance of the Wright brothers' first flight.

Airplanes continually improved during World War II, and they flew faster, farther, and higher than ever before. Nearly all planes of this era used **piston engines**, gasoline engines like the one Wilbur and Orville Wright put on their 1903 *Flyer*. A piston engine is similar to an automobile engine. In an automobile, the power from the engine drives wheels, while in an airplane, the power turns propellers.

The B-29 Superfortress showed just how powerful piston engines could be. The B-29 (*B* stands for bomber) was a huge and powerful plane with a top speed of about 350 mph. It could fly almost 4,000 miles nonstop on bombing missions over the Pacific Ocean.

The B-29 was the first airplane with pressurized crew compartments. At high altitudes the air pressure drops. Inside the B-29's crew compartments, people could breathe easily, because air was pumped in under pressure.

In 1945, two B-29s dropped the first atomic bombs on Japan. A long and complicated war had finally ended.

After the war, advances in military aircraft were used to improve civilian airliners. On the outside, airliners of the 1950s looked very much like wartime bombers and cargo planes. On the inside, they were large and luxurious planes that gave their passengers a comfortable ride.

The cabin in Lockheed's Constellation was pressurized, like the crew compartments of a B-29 bomber. And like the B-29, the Constellation could fly nonstop over continents and oceans.

Airliners such as the Constellation were the last of the large, piston-engined airplanes. The Constellation's engines were powerful, but they were heavy and complicated. The time was right for a new aircraft engine, the **jet**.

The Constellation, nicknamed the Connie, was comfortable and luxurious in spite of its resemblance to World War II bombers.

The T-33, the standard United States jet trainer of the 1950s, helped bring in the new jet age. The large openings on either side of the fuselage of this T-33 are air intakes. Air is drawn through the intakes into a chamber in the engine where it is compressed, or squeezed, and mixed with fuel. There the fuel mixture ignites and burns. When gases burn, they expand, or take up more room. The expanded gases shoot out the tail pipe, and the airplane shoots forward.

This action gives the F-80, the fighter version of the T-33, its nickname, Shooting Star. The F-80 Shooting Star was the first jet to be produced in large numbers in the United States. The F-80 had a cruising speed of 500 mph and won the first jet-to-jet air fight with a Soviet MiG-15.

This T-33 is painted in the colors of the Thunderbirds, the United States Air Force precision flying team.

Both the F-80 and the T-33 had tip tanks, fuel tanks on the ends of the wings. They were made to drop off when empty, but pilots discovered that the plane flew better with the tanks than without.

Later jets flew even faster than the T-33 and F-80, but there was a point around 700 mph where aircraft would shake and vibrate terribly. Planes approaching that speed would go out of control and would even break apart in flight. Sound travels at about 700 mph, so this invisible wall where planes went out of control was called the **sound barrier**.

Pilot Charles Yeager named this plane Glamorous Glennis after his wife. It was the first plane of the X, or experimental, series to fly faster than the speed of sound.

Engineers looked for ways to cut through the sound barrier. They studied the shape of a bullet, because bullets are **supersonic**, meaning they go faster than the speed of sound. The engineers built a bullet-shaped aircraft with a rocket engine like that used to launch a spacecraft. The engineers called the plane the Bell X-1. (X stands for experimental.)

In 1947, test pilot Charles Yeager flew the Bell X-1 through the sound barrier. The air filled with a loud noise, called a sonic boom, but the Bell X-1 did not break apart. The age of supersonic flight had arrived.

Right: *The cockpit of the F-86 Sabre was so crowded with instruments that some flyers complained there was no room left for the pilot.*

Only a few years after Yeager's flight in the Bell X-1, war broke out in Korea. The United States Air Force (USAF) wanted a jet fighter that could fly at the speed of sound. The F-86 Sabre, the United States' first supersonic jet fighter, flew its first mission in Korea in 1950. The Sabre's wings were swept back at an angle to reduce drag. Pilots found the jet to be unstable at very high speeds and most often flew their Sabres at just under the speed of sound for better control.

In Korea, Sabre jets flew against Soviet-made MiG-15s. The MiGs and the Sabres were evenly matched, but the American pilots were more experienced and won most of the air battles.

This Sikorsky S-76 air rescue helicopter carries medical supplies and paramedics ready to take care of injured and sick people in flight.

Helicopters played an important part in the Korean War and again in later wars. On helicopters, **rotors** replace the wings of other types of aircraft. These rotors look and act like propellers, turning constantly when the aircraft is in flight. Rotors lift the helicopter from the ground, allow it to hover in one place, and push it through the air.

Because helicopters can take off and land straight up and down in small spaces, they are very useful in rescue work. Helicopters were first used on a small scale during World War II. In Korea, Vietnam, and the war in the Persian Gulf, they went behind enemy lines to rescue the wounded. In peacetime, they are used by police for search-and-rescue missions, for radio and television reporting, for traffic updating, for crop dusting, and for many other jobs.

Helicopters are not the only aircraft that can get in and out of tight places. Bush planes are small, rugged airplanes that fly in remote areas of the world, where there may not be roads or runways. Bush planes are often fitted with floats for landing on water or skis for landing on snow.

Early in the 1950s, the deHavilland Company asked bush pilots what kind of airplane they would design if they had the chance. Pilots said they wanted a reliable airplane with enough lift for short takeoffs and with plenty of room for cargo. DeHavilland built the Beaver with these requests in mind. Although it is not made anymore, it is still the most popular airplane with bush pilots.

In the 1960s, the United States went into combat in the Southeast Asian nation of Vietnam. There, many United States pilots flew big, powerful F-4 Phantom jets.

The Phantom's engines provided so much thrust that the F-4 could go straight up during climbs. During level flight, the F-4 reached a top speed of one and one-half times the speed of sound, or **Mach** 1.5. (Mach measures speeds at or beyond the speed of sound. Mach 1 is about 700 mph, while Mach 2 is two times the speed of sound, or about 1,400 mph.)

When the F-4 was first put into action, it was armed only with air-to-air missiles. Shooting guns from supersonic fighters was thought to be out-of-date. The F-4's pilots disagreed with this, and the jet was later fitted with guns.

F-4 pilots in Vietnam first trained in T-38 Talons. The T-38 was the United States' first supersonic trainer and is still one of the few being used worldwide. The Talon has been used by the USAF Thunderbirds and by the United States Navy in its Top Gun training program. NASA astronauts use Talons to keep up their flight skills.

In the two-seat T-38 Talon, the instructor's seat is raised for a view over the shoulder of the student pilot.

Pilots and flight engineer prepare for takeoff on the flight deck of a 727 airliner.

While military airplanes flew at the speed of sound and beyond, airliners joined the jet age. In the mid-1950s, the Boeing Company introduced its 707th airplane design, the 707 jet airliner. It had a cruising speed of 600 mph and flew higher than earlier piston-engined airliners. Flying at higher altitudes gives passengers a smoother ride, because they are flying "above the weather."

The 707 was soon followed by the 727. The first 727 rolled out of the factory in 1962. The 727 has three jet engines mounted at the tall, T-shaped tail. Its bullet-shaped nose and swept-back wings reduce drag for higher speeds. The 727's wings are arched to give the plane more lift. More lift helps the plane take off on short runways.

In the 1960s, more people were flying, and airports were becoming crowded. Some people thought air traffic could be reduced by building larger airliners. In 1969, the first jumbo jet, the Boeing 747, was introduced.

The 747 was twice as heavy as any earlier airliner. It carries 500 passengers, nearly five times as many passengers as a 727.

In 1989 Boeing brought out the 747-400.

This plane is so big, that when it is on the runway the cockpit is 30 feet above the ground. If the 747-400 were a building, the pilot would be looking out of a third-story window. Passengers on the 747-400's upper and lower decks enjoy a smooth ride, even at a cruising speed of 550 mph. Pilots like the 747-400 because it is so large that it is not affected by turbulence, or rough air.

A 747-400 being prepared for takeoff

While airliners were flying at ever higher altitudes, a remarkable military plane, the SR-71, was flying at the very edge of space. It flew so high its pilots wore space suits. The SR-71, introduced in 1964, regularly flew at speeds over Mach 3, faster than a speeding bullet. It was made of titanium, a strong, lightweight metal that can withstand the very high heat of supersonic flight.

The SR-71 was a **stealth** aircraft. Stealth aircraft are hard to see, hear, or pick up on radar. Nicknamed the Blackbird, the SR-71 was painted black so it couldn't be seen flying at night. Although it was a large aircraft, it was so "radar slippery" that it only made a small blip on radar screens.

The SR-71 was used as a spy plane until 1990. From 18 miles up, the Blackbird's cameras took such detailed photos that you could read the numbers on a license plate.

On its last flight, the SR-71 Blackbird broke speed records by flying from Los Angeles to Washington, D.C., in just over an hour. Its average speed on this flight was over 2,000 mph.

A popular plane with pilots, the F-16 Flying Falcon uses an electronic system called fly-by-wire for flight control. This jet fighter has so many electronic systems and computers on board that it has been called the Electric Jet.

In 1991, the F-16 Falcon was used in the war in the Persian Gulf as a fighter and attack jet. F-16s also made reconnaissance flights, scouting for tanks dug into the desert sand.

Pilots love to fly the Falcon. One pilot said, "The visibility when you're flying is unbelievable. You don't feel like you're in the airplane. You feel like you're part of it, or it's part of you."

"This isn't an airplane you climb into," says one
F-16 pilot. *"This is an airplane you strap on!"*

Very few pilots have had a chance to fly anything like the X-29, an experimental airplane first flown in 1984. The X-29 is the first American airplane to fly successfully with forward-swept wings, wings that point to the front of the airplane. The X-29's wings are also made to bend and change shape. The tips of the wings actually twist during flight to make the plane easier to maneuver. Because of the X-29's success, more airplanes with forward-swept wings are being planned.

Aircraft designer Burt Rutan is working with new ideas, materials, and designs to change the way airplanes will look in the future. People all over the world learned about Rutan in 1986, when his brother Dick and copilot Jeana Yeager flew Rutan's *Voyager* airplane nonstop around the world without refueling.

The same year that the graceful, sailplane-like *Voyager* made its flight, Rutan built a test model for the Beechcraft Starship, a business jet. The Starship has two backward-facing **turboprop** engines. A turboprop is a jet engine that uses power from expanded gases to turn a propeller. Turboprops are quieter than other types of jet engines. They fly at lower altitudes and slower speeds, using less fuel than other jets. The Starship's turboprop engines are called pusher engines, because they push the plane through the air.

Computers were used to help design, build, test, maintain, and fly the Starship. The cockpit is sometimes called a glass flight deck, because many of the traditional flight instruments have been replaced by glass computer screens.

The Starship has a small wing at the front of the airplane called a **canard wing**. The canard wing and **winglets**, turned-up ends on the main wings, help stabilize the plane in flight. The airplane is made mainly of strong, lightweight combinations of graphite and epoxy. These combinations of materials are called **composites**.

As time goes on, the Wright brothers' 1903 *Flyer* seems even more amazing. The wings of the *Flyer* twisted like those of the latest experimental aircraft, the X-29. The Wright brothers controlled the wing tips with wires instead of computers. Burt Rutan's "new" forward canard wing is a modern version of a Wright brothers' design. The Wrights put the tail of their *Flyer* in front of the wings for stability. Other airplanes, such as the Starship, have used pusher engines, but the *Flyer* was the first airplane with backward-facing engines and propellers. The history of the airplane is the story of constant refinements of existing designs. In the end, it all comes back to the original dream of flying. To the pure, personal joy of flight.

Glossary

barnstormers: pilots who performed stunts in the air, offered rides for a fee, and entertained people across the country with their flying skills after World War I

biplane: an airplane with two sets of wings, one above the other. The 1903 Wright *Flyer*, the first successful motorized airplane, was a biplane.

canard wing: a small wing found at the front of an airplane. In Burt Rutan's Starship, the canard wing helps give the airplane stability.

cockpit: sometimes called the flight deck, an area within an airplane's fuselage for the pilot, crew, and flight controls

composites: building materials made by combining two or more substances under heat and pressure. Composites are generally super-strong and lightweight.

cowlings: smooth metal coverings for the engine. In early airplanes, cowlings not only reduced drag but also kept oil from flying onto pilots.

drag: resistance to forward motion. By lowering wing flaps pilots increase drag, making it possible to land at a slow, safe speed.

fuselage: the body of an aircraft, extending from the nose to the tail, but not including parts that project from the plane

jet: a type of engine. Jet engines draw in air, compress it, add fuel, burn the mixture, and use the fast-flowing exhaust gases for thrust.

lift: the upward force created when air flows over and around curved wings. Lift and thrust work against drag and the pull of gravity to get an airplane off the ground.

light airplanes: lightweight, single-engined airplanes with many uses, including pilot training, crop dusting, traveling, and flying for fun

Before the SR-71 Blackbird went on its first mission, the sailplanelike U-2 was America's most famous spy plane.

The most popular United States fighter plane of World War II, the P-51 is still used today for racing and aerobatic demonstrations.

Mach: a measurement for speeds at or beyond the speed of sound. At Mach 1, an airplane is flying at the speed of sound, or about 700 mph. Mach 2 is twice the speed of sound.

monoplane: an airplane with a single set of wings, where each wing is attached to opposite sides of the fuselage

navigation: finding the way from one place to another. Early pilots compared what they saw on the ground to road maps, while modern pilots rely on radar, computers, and other systems.

piston engines: gasoline-powered engines used in motorcycles, automobiles, and many airplanes beginning with the Wright *Flyer*.

propellers: long, twisted blades powered by airplane engines. Propellers act like constantly spinning wings.

reconnaissance: in wartime, looking for and checking the position of enemy troops

sound barrier: an imaginary wall encountered by pilots when flying at the speed of sound

stealth: the quality of being hard to see. *Stealth* is often used to describe airplanes that cannot be detected with radar.

struts: supporting pieces that help make an airplane strong and sturdy. On most biplanes, struts connect upper and lower wings.

supersonic: anything that travels faster than the speed of sound, which is about 700 mph

thrust: the force which causes an airplane to move forward

turboprop: a kind of engine that combines features of a jet with a propeller. While turboprops are slower than standard jet engines, they use less fuel and are quieter.

winglets: small, upturned ends on the main wings. On the 747-400, winglets help keep the airplane stable in flight.

Index

Acknowledgments

The author wishes to thank: Robert, Brendt, and Barry Taylor
at the Airpower Museum; the Antique Airplane Association;
Stu Almleaf; Tony Bour and the others at the Minnesota Air-
guard Museum; Dale Anderson and all the other Colonels of
the Southern Minnesota Wing of the Confederate Airforce;
Ray Mabrey; Mary Hastings; Al Lange at Elliott Beechcraft;
Wipaire; T/Sgt. James Goodall; the South Dakota Air and Space
Museum; Ross Sublett; the 148th Fighter Interceptor Group
of the Minnesota Air National Guard; and very special thanks
to Sherm Booen.

Photo Acknowledgments

All photos by the author except the following, which are repro-
duced through the courtesy of: pp. 6 (top), 11, 30, Smithsonian
Institution; p. 6 (bottom), Deutsches Museum; pp. 8, 9, 45,
Library of Congress; p. 15, Minnesota Historical Society; p. 18,
Bettmann Archive; p. 35 (bottom), James C. Goodall; p. 37,
H. N. Bullock for Northwest Airlines; p. 38, Lockheed Aero-
nautical Systems Co.; p. 39, George Pennick, from the collection
of James C. Goodall; p. 42, Grumman Corporation. Author
photo on back jacket flap by Rick Moulton.